574.526

LEICESTERSHIRE
COUNTY COUNCIL
LIBRARIES AND
INFORMATION SERVICE

Bown
Deri

Field + Hedgerow.

THROUGH THE SEASONS

Field and Hedgerow

Deni Bown

Illustrated by Mike Atkinson

Through the Seasons

Field and Hedgerow
Garden
Park
Pond
Stream
Wood

Edited by Philippa Smith
Series design by Charles Harford HSD
Book design by Ross George

First published in 1989 by
Wayland (Publishers) Ltd
61 Western Road, Hove
East Sussex BN3 1JD, England

British Library Cataloguing in Publication Data
Bown, Deni
   1. Great Britain. Fields & hedgerows.
Organisms
   I. Title II. Atkinson, Mike III. Series
   574.941

ISBN 1 85210 758 8

Phototypeset by DP Press, Sevenoaks, Kent
Printed in Italy by G. Canale & C.S.p.A., Turin
Bound in Belgium by Casterman S.A.

CONTENTS

Words that appear in **bold** in the text
are explained in the glossary on page 30.

Much of our countryside is made up of fields and hedges.

Farmland is divided into fields which are used for growing crops, rearing **livestock**, and producing **hay** and **silage.** Most fields are surrounded by hedges. A hedge is a row of **shrubs** planted to protect the field from strong winds, to keep the livestock in and to mark the boundaries of each piece of land. Most hedges are trimmed regularly but some are left to become wild and overgrown. Many plants and animals live in the shelter of hedges. The numbers in fields vary greatly, depending on the kind of field. Those with the most are **meadows** which have not been ploughed for many years.

The hedge on the right has been taken out to make the corn field bigger. ▶

Removing hedges gives more room for crops but means the loss of many plants and animals. Between 1946 and 1974, over 200,000 km of hedges in Britain were destroyed. Some parts of the country changed greatly and are no longer as rich in wildlife, or as beautiful as they were.

◀ There are special ways of making and trimming hedges.

A **traditional** laid hedge can be seen at the front of the picture. Laid hedges are made by cutting half way through the main stems of the shrubs, close to the base, and bending them to one side in neat layers. Then a row of strong stakes, leaning in the opposite direction, is driven in to support the bent stems. Lastly, the tops of the stakes are bound together with hazel or willow branches.

There are many different kinds of hedges.

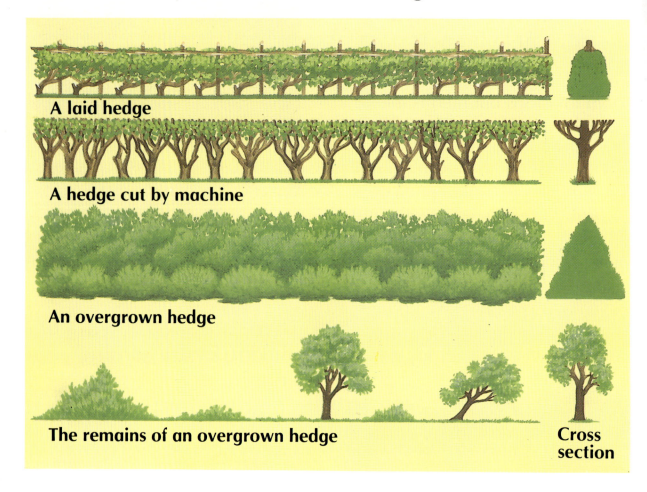

A laid hedge

A hedge cut by machine

An overgrown hedge

The remains of an overgrown hedge

Cross section

At one time, all hedges were laid and trimmed by hand. It was hard work and needed a great deal of skill. A skilled hedger could lay over 25 m of hedge in a day. Even then, it might take him the whole winter to lay all the hedges on a farm.

Nowadays, it is very expensive to look after hedges by hand. Most are either cut by **flails** attached to tractors or are neglected. A wild hedge gradually becomes bare at the base and turns into a line of separate shrubs and trees.

guelder rose

spindle

traveller's joy

elder

field maple

crab apple

There are many shrubs and climbers in old hedgerows.

Some hedges are hundreds of years old. It is possible to find out roughly how old a hedge is by counting the number of different shrubs, not including climbing plants, in a stretch of 30 paces (about 25 m). Each different kind represents about 125 years of growth. Before working out the age, you need to know what the different kinds of shrubs look like.

Hawthorn is the most common hedgerow shrub.

At one time, farmland was divided into very large areas which were shared by the farmers. In the eighteenth century, it was declared by law that the land should be divided between the farmers and properly enclosed by fences, ditches and hedges of quickset (another name for hawthorn). Many hawthorn hedges date from this time.

◄ Hawthorn flowers are called may blossom.

Hawthorn hedges make a thick network of spiny branches which is difficult for animals to get through. All parts of hawthorn are useful to wildlife. Birds nest in the branches and eat the fruits. Insects feed on the scented flowers. Many different moths and butterflies lay eggs on its leaves, which provide food for the caterpillars.

Blackthorn is the first hedgerow shrub to flower in spring.

In early spring, the blackthorn bushes are white with blossom. The flowers appear on the black, spiny branches before the new leaves. The fruits of the blackthorn are called sloes. They look like small blue-grey plums but they are very bitter.

Primroses grow on damp sunny banks.

Primrose plants grow mainly in the winter and early spring when the surrounding **vegetation** has died down. They are in full flower during the spring, though one or two flowers may be found at any time during the winter, especially in mild weather. The flowers stay open night and day, even in rain or snow.

The bright flowers of red campion attract moths.

Most insects cannot see red colours but moths can. The lychnis moth flies from flower to flower, feeding on **nectar** and laying a single egg in some of the flowers. As it does so, it picks up **pollen** on its body from the male flowers which later falls on to a female flower. When this happens, the seeds of the female flower begin to develop. The moth's eggs hatch within a week and the caterpillars feed on the growing seeds. Although the moth damages the plant, it **pollinates** more flowers than it destroys.

Celandines open wide in the sunshine and close tightly when it rains.

Damp sunny places along hedgerow ditches are often covered in celandines. The new heart-shaped leaves come up in early spring, soon followed by the flowers. Like buttercups, they have glossy petals. The ladybird in the picture has come out of **hibernation** now that the weather has become warmer.

10

The flowers of lords-and-ladies trap flies.

Jack-by-the-hedge is also called garlic mustard.

The leaves of jack-by-the-hedge smell strongly of garlic. At one time they were gathered from the hedgerows to put into salads or to make a sauce for fish or mutton, which gave it another name – 'sauce alone'.

The tiny flowers are hidden in a chamber below the green hood. They smell like **dung** to attract flies. The flies land on the hood and fall into the chamber, where they are imprisoned until the flowers are pollinated. The female flowers then develop into a cluster of poisonous berries which turn red in late summer.

◀ Stitchwort is found in grassy places on sheltered banks.

Many wild flowers have 'wort' as part of their name, such as stitchwort and figwort. It is a word that was once given to plants that could be used to cure illnesses. Stitchwort was made into a medicine to treat a pain (or 'stitch') in the side.

More dandelions flower in spring than at any other time of year.

▶

Although a few dandelions can always be found in flower, they open in their thousands on warm sunny spring days. The flowers are followed by round heads of silky seeds. These are known as dandelion clocks from the children's game of blowing the seeds to find out what time it is. When ripe, the seeds are blown away by the wind. They land a long way from the parent plant so have plenty of room to grow.

Wrens build their nests and feed on insects in the hedge.

The male wren makes several nests so that the female has a choice of where to lay her eggs. He uses moss, leaves and grass which he collects from the hedgerow and weaves into a dome shape. Wrens are very small birds. In very cold weather, they huddle together to keep warm.

long-tailed tit

thrush

chaffinch

magpie

wood mouse

bank vole

NOT TO SCALE

weasel

The hedge provides food and protection for many animals.

Birds find insects, seeds and fruits in the hedgerow, as well as secret places to build their nests. Bank voles, wood mice and rabbits dig burrows close by, coming out at night to nibble the vegetation. Hedgehogs and shrews hunt in the undergrowth, feeding on small creatures such as insects, worms, snails and spiders. The same kind of **prey** is enjoyed by frogs and slow worms which live in damp ditches at the foot of the bank. Tawny owls, weasels and stoats are the main hedgerow **predators**. They seize mice, voles, rabbits and birds. Weasels are small enough to go down narrow burrows after their prey. Both weasels and stoats steal eggs from nests.

THINGS TO DO IN SPRING

Think of a hedgerow that you can visit several times through the spring and summer. Make your own 'flora' of the hedgerow. A flora is a record of all the different plants which grow in a particular place.

A collection of pressed flowers.

To do this you will need to collect just one leaf or flowering stem from each kind of plant and press it. If you have a proper flower press, you can use that. If not, the leaves and flowers can be pressed between pages of an old telephone directory, or between sheets of newspaper with heavy books on top of them. Make sure your **specimens** are quite dry before you press them, and take great care to lay them as flat as possible when you put the top piece of paper in position. They will take several weeks to dry out.

When the specimens are quite dry, they can be mounted in a scrap book using thin strips of Sellotape or small dabs of glue. Dried leaves and flowers are very fragile, and you will need to handle them with great care. As you mount each one, try to find out what it is and label it neatly. A book of wild flowers will help you **identify** your specimens.

◀ **Drifts of cow parsley line the hedgerow in early summer.**

Cow parsley reaches 1.5 m when flowering. The tiny white flowers are grouped together in flat-topped heads. These show up well from a distance and provide wide landing platforms for several insects at a time. The insects pollinate the flowers as they move about on the flowerhead, feeding on nectar and pollen.

The scented flowers of the dog rose last only a few days.

▶

Dog roses have long arching stems covered in downward-pointing thorns. The thorns catch on the surrounding vegetation and hold the stems in place as they climb upwards.

Goosegrass has hooked bristles which help it climb into the hedge.

The stems of goosegrass (or cleavers, as it is also called) are very weak. The only way it can grow upwards is by clinging to other plants. The small round seeds have hooked bristles too. They stick to fur and clothing, travelling long distances before they land somewhere and start to grow. Goosegrass used to be fed to geese to fatten them.

◄ Honeysuckle flowers have a strong scent at night to attract moths.

Honeysuckle is a climber which winds tightly round the stems of other plants. Its tube-shaped flowers have nectar deep inside. The moths reach the nectar with their long tongues and pollinate the flowers as they feed.

six-spot
burnet
moth

burying beetle

common blue
butterfly

meadow
cranesbill

false oat
grass

grasshopper

red
clover

couch
grass

birdsfoot trefoil

plantain

NOT TO SCALE

The meadow is a jungle of grasses and flowers.

The number of different plants and animals in a meadow depends on its age. Years ago meadows were grazed by livestock and cut for hay but otherwise left alone. This gave more **sensitive** plants and animals time to become **established**. Nowadays, most meadows are grown as a **fodder** crop by the farmer who sows seeds of quick-growing plants. They are grazed, cut for hay or silage and ploughed up every few years so that another crop can be planted. Only tough, common plants and animals are found in short-lived meadows.

Buttercups are the most common flowers in summer meadows.

Although buttercups look bright yellow to us, they appear purple to bees. The eyes of insects are not the same as ours. We have one large **lens**, but most insects have many tiny lenses joined together. They see some colours differently and are ten times faster at noticing movement.

◀ Cuckoo spit is made by young froghoppers.

Froghoppers are insects which suck plant juices. They are called froghoppers because they jump and have broad heads, which make them look a bit like frogs. The females lay eggs on plants in the autumn which hatch the following spring. The delicate young froghoppers surround themselves with a mass of bubbles as a protection against their enemies and hot sunshine.

◀ Shieldbugs suck the juices from nettle leaves.

Many different insects feed on nettles. Butterflies such as red admirals, peacocks, commas and small tortoiseshells lay eggs on nettles and their caterpillars eat the leaves. Nettle leaves are covered in stiff hollow hairs. When touched they inject an **acid** into your skin which makes it sting.

The hedge brown butterfly is seen along hedgerows in summer. ▶

The female hedge brown lays her eggs one at a time on blades of grass. They hatch in about three weeks and the caterpillars feed at night until the autumn. When the weather turns cold, they hibernate low down among the grasses. In the spring, they start feeding again until they are fully grown. Then they turn into **chrysalises** which become butterflies a few weeks later.

Soldier beetles feed on the smaller insects. ▶

Orangey-red and black soldier beetles are common on meadow and hedgerow flowers. They prey upon insects that have come to feed on nectar and pollen. Soldier beetles are also known as bloodsuckers because of their reddish colour. The colour acts as a warning to birds that they are unpleasant to eat.

◀ **Hammock spiders wait beneath their webs to catch insects.**

The hammock spider spins a dense web which is slung between the twigs of hedgerow shrubs. It lurks upside down in the centre of the web until an insect gets tangled in the threads. Then it runs along and wraps the insect up in more threads so that it cannot escape. The webs are easy to spot in late summer and autumn when they are covered with dew.

Rabbits eat the grass at the edges of the field.

A slow worm is not a worm but a kind of lizard.

The large eyes and twitching ears of rabbits are always alert for danger. Rabbits have many enemies. Hawks, owls, stoats, weasels and foxes, as well as human beings, hunt them. They need plenty of places to hide and often dig their burrows along a hedgerow where they can dash for cover. Rabbits live together in a network of underground tunnels called a warren. It has many entrances. At dusk they venture out to begin feeding. They eat grass, **crops** and the bark of young trees.

Slow worms are legless lizards. Their skin is very smooth and shiny, like polished metal. Although they look like snakes, they are harmless slow-moving **reptiles**. They eat insects and worms but live mainly on slugs which they hunt at dusk or after rain. In late summer, the female gives birth to about a dozen gold-coloured babies which are only 5 cm long. They begin to look after themselves as soon as they are born. They eat insects until they are large enough to swallow slugs.

THINGS TO DO IN SUMMER

Continue to collect and press leaves and flowers for your hedgerow flora.

Try to work out the age the hedgerow you visit. If you have been collecting plant specimens since the spring, you will be able to identify most of the shrubs by now. Count only the shrubs (not the climbers) in a length of 30 paces, beginning about 10 paces from the end of the hedge. Each kind represents 125 years.

As there will probably be some variation, it is best to count three separate sections of the same hedge and divide the total number by three to get the average. You will probably find that hedges of hazel and maple are older than those which are mainly of hawthorn.

Draw a picture of a hedgerow at night under a full moon. Which animals become active at dusk, hunting and feeding when it is dark?

The dog rose and elder bloom in summer.

◀ **The dog rose has scarlet rosehips in the autumn.**

Hedgerow plants are laden with ripe fruits in the autumn. Rosehips are eaten by birds who spread the seeds along the hedgerow.

◀ **Blackberries are eaten by mice, voles and flies as well as birds.**

Most hedgerows have brambles. The fruits are eaten by hedgerow animals, as well as by people who gather them to make jam and puddings. The leaves are important too. The caterpillars of at least ten different kinds of moths feed on them, including the peach blossom moth. It gets its name from the large pale pink blotches on its brown wings. They **camouflage** it well against the bramble flowers.

THINGS TO DO IN AUTUMN

Hawthorn berries are called haws.

The most interesting thing about hedgerows in autumn is the number of different fruits and seeds. See how many of these you can collect: rosehips, blackberries, haws, sloes, crab apples, guelder rose berries, traveller's joy seedheads, hazel nuts, spindle berries, maple keys, holly berries, honeysuckle berries. Take a basket and a pair of scissors and cut just one cluster of each kind. Do not handle any berries. Although blackberries and hazel nuts are safe to eat, the others are unpleasant or poisonous to humans. When you have finished your harvest, try to identify them. When you have found out what they all are, put them out for the birds to eat.

Hedge-laying competitions are held every autumn. They are organized by the National Hedge-laying Society. You can find out about them through the nearest branch of the Young Farmers Club. Do go to see one if you can.

Holly berries often last right through the winter.

Holly bushes have either male or female flowers. For the female bush to bear berries, it must be growing near a male bush so that the pollen can be blown by the wind from the male to the female flowers. Holly is an **evergreen**. It keeps its leaves all through the year, losing old ones a few at a time and growing new ones in spring. The leaves are tough and shiny to prevent damage by frost and snow. They are also prickly to put animals off eating them.

Hazel catkins appear on the bare bushes at the end of winter.

Catkins are the male flowers which release pollen when the wind blows. It blows on to the female flowers and makes them grow into hazel nuts. The female flowers are very tiny red tufts which grow singly on the same branches as the catkins. Hazel bushes are **deciduous**, losing their leaves in the autumn and growing new ones each spring after flowering.

THINGS TO DO IN WINTER

From a distance, the hedgerow looks bare and lifeless in winter. If you walk slowly and look more closely, you will see many signs of life. Dead goosegrass plants hang on to the hedge throughout the winter. Beneath them you will find seedlings which **germinated** during the autumn.

Every twig has buds which are ready to open into new leaves and flowers when spring comes. The buds of each kind of plant are different. Ash buds are hard and sooty black. Blackthorn has groups of tiny round buds. Catkin buds can be seen on the hazel bushes. By late winter they lengthen and dangle as the flowers begin to open.

Some hedgerow plants put out new leaves in the winter. The first to be seen are the handsome arrow-shaped leaves of lords-and-ladies, which are often black-spotted. Soon afterwards you may see the feathery leaves of cow parsley. You may also find the first primrose or an early dandelion.

Some hedgerow animals hibernate. You may discover many ladybirds close together in a dead leaf, or the chrysalis of a butterfly. Birds, mice, voles and rabbits remain active and have to find food however cold the weather is. If you are very quiet, you may see some of them feeding.

Nature seems to be sleeping on frosty winter days.

27

Spring

Summer

Autumn

Winter

GLOSSARY

Acid A sour-tasting liquid which stings if applied to wounds.

Camouflage Colouring which makes an animal blend in with its surroundings.

Chrysalises Hardened cases in which insect grubs change into adults (for example, caterpillars into butterflies).

Crops Food plants grown by farmers, such as vegetables and corn.

Deciduous Losing all the leaves at the end of the growing season.

Dung Waste matter passed by animals.

Established Settled, permanent.

Evergreen Bearing leaves throughout the year.

Flails Hedge cutters attached to a tractor.

Fodder Food for livestock.

Germinate To begin to grow (for example, seeds).

Hay A mixture of dried grasses and other meadow plants which is used to feed livestock during the winter.

Hibernation Going into a sleep-like state during the winter.

Identify To find out the name.

Lens The part of the eye that focuses beams of light.

Livestock Farm animals (for example, sheep and cows).

Meadows Grassland used for grazing and making hay or silage.

Nectar A sugary liquid produced by flowers.

Pollen Powder produced by the male parts of a flower which makes the female parts develop seeds.

Pollinate To carry pollen from the male parts of a flower to the female parts.

Predators Animals which kill other animals for food.

Prey An animal which is killed by another for food.

Reptiles A group of animals that have backbones, scaly skin and short or no legs (for example, snakes and lizards).

Sensitive Easily affected by changes or disturbances.

Shrubs Woody plants which are smaller than trees and have branches close to ground level.

Silage A fodder crop which is cut and stored in special containers (called silos) for feeding to livestock in winter.

Specimen An example which shows what something is like.

Traditional Used to describe a custom which has been carried out in the same way for hundreds of years.

Vegetation Plant life.

BOOKS TO READ

Butterflies and Moths by Anne Smith (Wayland, 1990).

The Children's Book of the Countryside (Usborne, 1977).

Discovering Hedgehogs by Elizabeth Bomford (Wayland, 1985).

Discovering Weasels by Miranda MacQuitty (Wayland, 1989).

The Life Cycle of a Ladybird by Jill Bailey (Wayland, 1989).

The Life Cycle of a Rabbit by John Williams (Wayland, 1988).

The Meadow Year by Irmgard Lucht (A. & C. Black, 1983).

The New Observer's Book of Wild Flowers by Francis Rose (Frederick Warne, 1978).

Spotter's Guide to Wild Flowers by Christopher Humphries (Usborne, 1978).

The Wildlife of Farmland by David Gilman (Macdonald, 1983).

Picture acknowledgements

All photographs were taken by Deni Bown with the exception of the following: Chris Fairclough Colour Library 13, 19 (below), 21 (both), 22 (right), 27; A.E. Wills 22 (left).

INDEX